GRATEFULLY DEADICATED PIN ART Coloring Book

Art by Gary Kroman
with Leslie D. Kippel

Backbeat Books

An Imprint of Hal Leonard LLC

T0351723

Published in 2017 by Backbeat Books
An Imprint of Hal Leonard LLC
7777 West Bluemound Road
Milwaukee, WI 53213

Trade Book Division Editorial Offices
33 Plymouth St., Montclair, NJ 07042

Printed in the United States of America

ISBN 978-1-4950-7674-9

www.backbeatbooks.com

Introduction

I began the First Free Underground Grateful Dead Tape Exchange in 1971. We recorded and traded live Grateful Dead concert tapes for free. As the popularity of trading live concerts on tape increased, a practice the Grateful Dead allowed and ultimately encouraged, I realized that I needed a more streamlined method of getting tapers together to trade. I started a newsletter to help my fellow tape traders connect, rather than all of them having to go through me. I came up with the name *Dead Relix*, because each Dead tape was a relic.

During the summer of 1973, I went to Bliss Park in Brooklyn, New York, to see a local Deadhead band, Sundance. Sitting on the ground with an artist pad, drawing a picture of the musicians, was Gary Kroman. I sat next to Gary and asked, "Hey . . . Can you draw a headlight on a northbound train going through the cool, cool Colorado rain?"

Gary went on to create volumes of art for *Relix* magazine. In the 1980s, Relix International, a new merchandising arm of *Relix* magazine, started to create cloisonné pins for music fans throughout the world.

Pin art quieted down in the 1990s, only to start up again within the past five years. It can currently be found at almost every concert, and collectors search high and low for desirable pins.

This coloring book is but a small sampling of the volumes of the magnificent pin art that has evolved over the years and is our way of sharing with you the process of creation! So get your pens and pencils ready, and color away!

Leslie D. Kippel
Founder, *Dead Relix*

710 ASHBURY

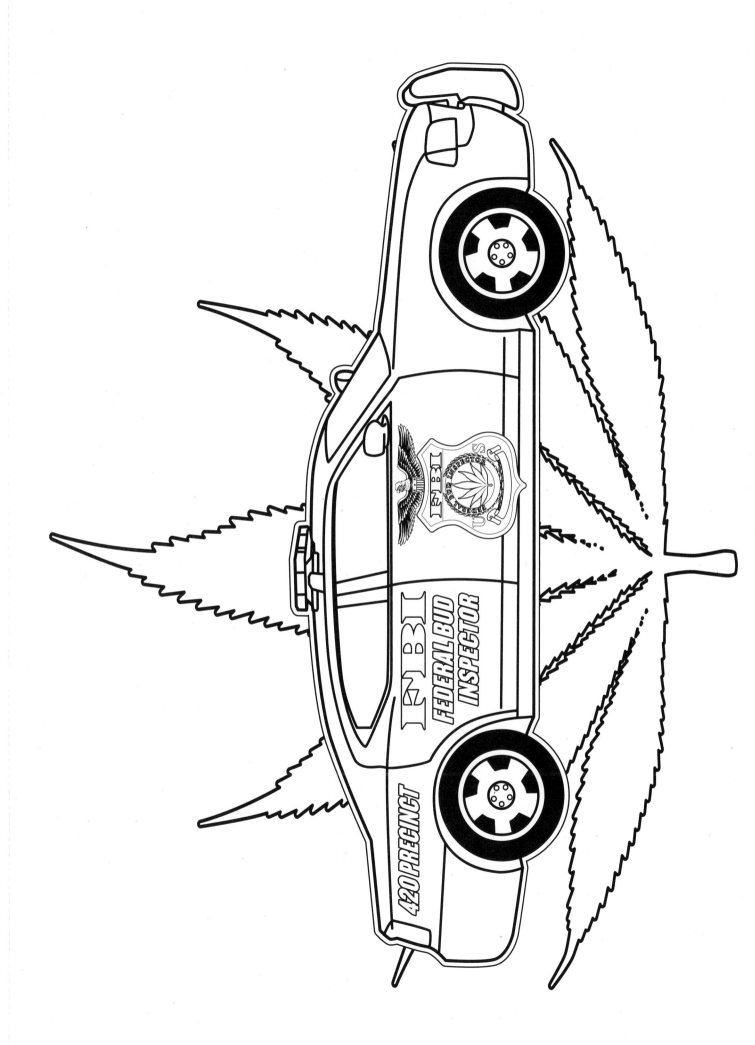

HUMBOLDT GROWERS ASSOCIATION

AMERICA'S FAVORITE GROWERS FOR 50 YEARS

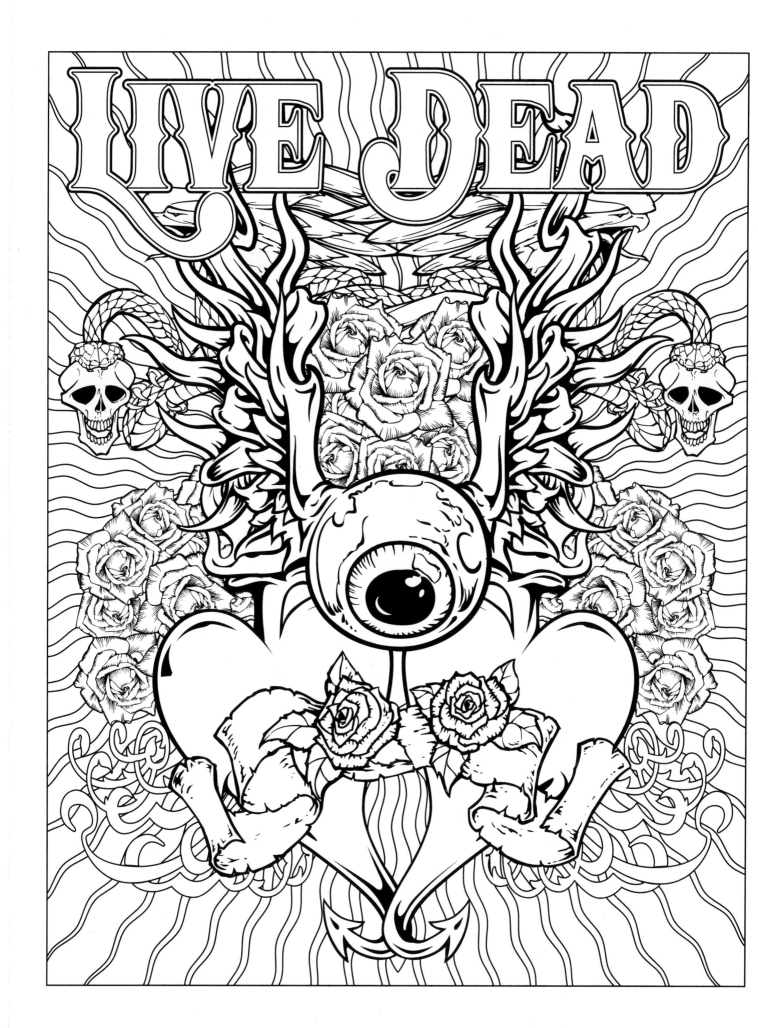

AN AMERICAN TRADITION